NEVER *be the* SAME

*"In all thy ways acknowledge Him,
and He shall direct thy paths."*
Proverbs 3:6 (KJV)

"Find your way."
Mark LeBlanc

NEVER *be the* SAME

MARK LeBLANC

with Terri Langhans

Scripture taken from King James Version is marked (KJV).

Photo credits:
Pages 108-114 author's collection
Page 114, top photo © Eric Weber
Page 115 © Jimi Allen Productions

Design by Jimi Allen Productions. www.jimiallen.com

ISBN 13: 978-1-931945-01-1
ISBN 10: 1-931945-01-2

Library of Congress Catalog Number: 2009938593

Printed in the United States of America

First Printing: April 2010

11 10 09 08 07   5 4 3 2 1

Expert Publishing, Inc.
14314 Thrush Street NW
Andover, MN 55304-3330
Andover, 1-877-755-4966
Minnesota www.expertpublishinginc.com

To the lights in my life

Tyler, Tracy, Trista, Janae,
Dominic, Clara, Sean, Michael,
Berit, and Selma

TABLE OF CONTENTS

INTRODUCTION

You don't win silver. You lose gold.

Nike pulled its 1996 Olympics ad that bore that headline after being criticized it went against the spirit of the Olympics. Yet, ironically, the concept came from Nike's understanding of the competitive spirit, from an insight the athletes themselves had voiced. On some level, many said, silver is second best. Close, but yet so far.

Unless you were on the Jamaican bobsled team in the 1988 Winter Olympics in Calgary, Alberta.

The five men and their coach won hearts worldwide, and they never even finished their race, let alone won a medal. In fact, I'll bet there are more people who remember the team's crash—and the endearing way they trotted to the finish line carrying their sled—than there are people who can remember who won the gold medal that year.

Of course the world wanted the Jamaican team to win. But that's not why the world cheered. It wasn't about winning. It was about being the best—not best on the planet, however. It was about achieving their personal best, as individuals and as a team. They couldn't lose. When you compare yourself to someone else, when you measure your performance by a medal (literally or metaphorically), you always lose. The world recognized and celebrated that fact in 1988 with the Jamaican bobsled team.

How soon we forget.

It took me a long time to realize that to have success in any area of my life, I did not have to be the best; I just had to do my best. Like the Jamaican bobsled team, I had a dream, yet completely and thoroughly blew it. Unlike the Jamaican bobsled team, I retreated like a frightened turtle, abandoned my dream, and almost let it die. I had not heard of, let alone grasped, the concept of personal best.

The Jamaican bobsled team rejoiced in their efforts, despite the outcome. They could have quit after the 1988 Olympics, but they didn't. They worked hard, on a consistent basis, and focused on the actions and activities that would keep them moving in the direction of their dream. Four years later, in 1992, they not only completed their races, they placed fourteenth—beating the U.S., French, Russian, and Italian teams.

What a story. Perhaps you saw the movie it inspired—*Cool Runnings,* starring John Candy. Personal best personified, if you ask me, although the producers never promoted it that way. I, on the other hand, like so many others, spent a lifetime attached to the outcome—the finish line, the win, the applause, the contract, the sale, the check, my credentials.

Don't get me wrong; I'm both proud and humbled by my accomplishments, including my first book, *Growing Your Business*. I am humbled by the many, many readers who have told me the positive impact it (and I) have had, and continue to have, on their business and success. And here's the part that always makes me smile. People know from my bio that I don't have a college degree, that I was not CEO of a Fortune Big Number company, that I don't have a string of initials or abbreviations after my name, and I've never been on *Oprah*. In other words, I don't have any of the medals, trophies, or trappings you'd expect from a guy who's made his living helping people start and grow successful businesses.

So, how is it an ordinary person like me has managed to do some seemingly extraordinary things, and helped others do the same? I used to answer that question (and, yes, people do ask it) by saying something about decades of trial and error, lessons learned the hard way in the entrepreneurial world of starting, running, and selling my own small business and helping others start or grow theirs. And while that answer is still entirely true, I know better now.

There's so much more to that story—two stories, actually. One that spans forty-eight years of success and failure, love and loss, sadness and joy, pain and healing. Another that spans five hundred miles and more than a million steps across Northern Spain—a story unto itself, many would say. But no, I don't think so, because one story could not be written without the other, and I can only tell them because of each other.

I hope you will enjoy, learn, and profit from the personal and professional lessons told here. I hope even more that both stories, woven together as I have, create a turning point in your life, perhaps inspiring a quest for your own personal best, one that takes you in the direction of your dream—to a path filled with meaning, success, happiness, and peace.

May you never be the same.

On the Bench

If only I spoke French, perhaps I wouldn't have been surprised. I'd still be in pain, out of breath, and ready to forever retire my hiking shoes and walking sticks, but at least I wouldn't have been so surprised.

I began my trek in St. Jean Pied de Port, a quaint river town with sandstone walls encircling what is essentially one main street, about eight kilometers (five miles) from the Spanish border.

Turns out that St. Jean Pied de Port, in English, translates "Saint John at the foot of the mountain pass," with foot being the operative word, and mountain being one of the Pyrenees. That name alone has a daunting ring to it, compared to the Poconos, anyway. The Pyrenees are nature's massive divider between France and Spain, and for me, they were the ultimate test of my stamina and spirit, not to mention my sanity.

If you think about it, hiking is usually somewhat of a happy word. But I was not hiking, nor happy. I was trudging, up and up and up a seemingly endless mountain road. In the rain. Every body part and vital organ voiced a complaint before the first hour had passed. Did I mention the rain? My thighs burned, I could barely breathe, and my heart pounded—in my ears! *Please, God, I need to rest.* Standing still, leaning on my hiking poles didn't help. I'd have given anything to sit down.

Did I mention the rain? I couldn't just sit in the dirt because a) it was mud, and b) I didn't want to re-enact a real-life version of the "I've fallen and I can't get up" shtick.

I prayed for a rock—no, make it a boulder—to be just around the corner. OK, the next corner. Maybe this corner? I started to feel sorry for myself and fantasize.

This is not the middle of nowhere. I am one of many walkers to pass this way. You'd think somebody would have rigged up a place to rest by now. . . . If I were a farmer along this road, I would surely put up a bench upon which travelers could rest. . . .I'd put it right here. . .right now. Ahhh, how nice would that be?

About one hundred yards later, indeed around the very next corner, I started hallucinating. Or was it a miracle? It looked like a bench.

It was real.

I plopped myself down, took off my pack, and collapsed. Apparently I wasn't the first one to seek respite here, nor the first to underestimate the severity of this adventure. Clothing and other items deemed unnecessary or expendable by previous travelers were randomly strewn about, as if the bargain table in a second-hand store had exploded.

What had I gotten myself into? What did these people know that I didn't? How could I get out of it? And that's when it hit me.

I still had 498 miles to go.

CHAPTER ONE

Stages

Twice I have appeared on stage in my underwear.

The first time was in junior high. The second was thirty-four years later, on a dare. Everyone else in the seventh grade in Fertile, Minnesota, was horrified at the thought of talking in front of the speech class, but I relished the opportunity. Robert Rickey, my teacher, must have seen something in me, sensed my long-held, albeit hidden, desire to be a performer of some sort. He believed in me, encouraged me, and pushed me at every turn.

I nailed the introductory speech on the topic of, well, me, and held my peers' rapt attention throughout my informative speech on the Vatican, of all things. In fact, after that presentation, Mr. Rickey asked me to perform in a skit. On a stage. With an older woman—a ninth grader named Kathy Schuske.

I was Adam; she was Eve. The play was *The Diary of Adam and Eve*, drawn from a short story by Mark Twain. It was a sweet little comedy where Adam was pretty much a low-key, whatever kind of guy trying to enjoy the estate, as he called it, until Eve, the new, long-haired creature shows up and wants to organize his life and talk, talk, talk. . . about us.

She re-names the estate "The Garden of Eden" and insists that Adam come up with names for all the animals. Fine.

"Swimmer, crawler, flyer, walker," my idiotic Adam declares, pointing to the imaginary animals. She, of course, rattles off something intelligently specific like walleye, tarantula, parrot, and goat.

We were hilarious and received many encore bookings in the community. The last time we performed the skit was on the main stage at Fertile-Beltrami High School to a packed crowd that went crazy when I came out on stage wearing nothing but my underwear and a green paper cutout of a fig leaf.

Boxers or briefs, you wonder? Does it really make a difference when you're thirteen years old?

❀   ❀   ❀   ❀   ❀   ❀

Notes from my Introductory Speech:

BORN:

March 17, 1961, in Minneapolis, Minnesota. Middle name, Arnold. My mom's doctor was Irish and had only girls. He told my dad how lucky he was to have a son and to have him born on Saint Patrick's Day. My dad did not care what day it was. He was just happy to have a boy. I was happy not to be named Pat.

PARENTS:

Ralph and Lois. Dad was a little bit like Ralph Kramden, the Jackie Gleason character on the old *The Honeymooners* television show. He was always thinking, always coming up with ideas, quite the entrepreneur. (Little did I know that my mother also had an entrepreneurial spirit. It would take forty years for me to find that out.)

SIBLINGS:

Older sister Sherry, younger sister Cathy, baby brother John.

SUMMERS:

Grandma and Grandpa Rude. (Ruby and Arnold.) Dairy farm in Fertile, Minnesota. Five-hour drive north. I had my BB gun, my fishing rod and reel, and a red Honda 50 mini-bike. Life was grand.

HOME:

Moved from Minneapolis to Fertile, population 968, when I was in fifth grade. Best day of my life. Church on Sunday at St. Joseph's Catholic Church without fail and no complaint.

FAVORITE FOOD:

Tater Tot hot dish.

FAVORITE SPORT:

Basketball.

* * * * * *

I am what most people would call average height. Always was. Back in elementary school and junior high, I can't remember anyone picking me out of a crowd and saying, "Hey, LeBlanc, look at you, Big Guy! You should be playing basketball."

One teacher did single me out for my size, however. In what might be considered a borderline tongue lashing, he told me in no uncertain terms that I had a better future in wrestling than basketball.

Bob Thorson was the assistant wrestling coach at my school, and he was known throughout the state for being the champion of young wrestlers, with a keen eye for talent and an incredible ability to coach and encourage. His belief in me helped me grow as an athlete and as a person, plus he set the stage for one of my first lessons in setting a goal and creating a plan to make something great happen.

In 1973, I was a lean, mean 119-pound-sixth grader, and I took first in the district and second in the regionals. I lost in the Amateur Athletic Union (AAU) State tournament, but my friend Eric Ellegaard became state champion and went on to place second in the national tournament.

That did it. My goal was set for the next year. I wanted to win the national title in my age group, and nothing would deter me from that goal. I practiced harder and longer than I ever had.

When the spring tournaments began, I won first in the district, placed second in the regionals, and came in second in the state tournament.

I won first and "placed" second? Did I just write that out loud?

I used my persuasive speech powers to get permission from the school to take their wrestling mats home for the summer and used them again to get permission from my parents to convert our basement into a wrestling room. My mom was worried about the smell, but my dad reminded her that basements, not to mention boys, are essentially born that way. I was worried about my sisters wanting to use the mats for slumber parties—or worse yet, dance and tumbling routines—but the smell factor worked in my favor on that issue.

I knew that my only chance of winning would be to practice with someone better than me, and that someone would have to be my friend Eric, the reigning state champion. I asked Eric if he'd be willing to train me; he said sure, and pounded me at every turn. I thought about wrestling—and winning—night and day, all year long.

When I returned the wrestling mats to school in the fall, my coach marveled at how well I had cared for them, and how clean and fresh they smelled. (Thanks, Mom.) He could also tell that I'd been training, and with his help, it paid off. I won first in the district, second in the regionals, which was good enough to get me a shot at the state title.

At thirteen years old, 133 pounds, I placed second in the Minnesota State Championships and went on to win the North Central U.S.A. title, which encompassed Minnesota, Wisconsin, Illinois, Iowa, North Dakota, South Dakota, and Indiana. It was the next best thing to winning the national title, and it was the national meet that was up next, all the way out west in California.

Unfortunately, we just couldn't afford to go.

But you know, I don't remember having more than a brief moment of regret. I did not realize it then; I didn't know what to call it, but I had just experienced the joy, relief, excitement, pride, accomplishment, satisfaction—you know what I mean—that comes from focusing, going all out, and achieving your dream. It was my personal best. It was amazing. And it was more than enough.

❅ ❅ ❅ ❅ ❅ ❅

My first job was hauling rubbish. I was nine years old, and, no, that does not mean my first job was as a garbage man. There's a big difference between rubbish and garbage, it turns out. The whole thing was my dad's idea. Always the consummate entrepreneur, even while he was employed full-time at Honeywell, Dad decided to start a business he could do evenings and weekends while still studying and starting his real estate business. Simply stated, he hauled rubbish to the dump. He bought a pickup truck and put an ad in the Minneapolis *Star Tribune*. My mom took the calls, created a schedule, and Dad took me with him on Saturdays and a few evenings. What an education! I would watch him size up a prospect, survey the stash to be hauled away from the basement or garage, give them a verbal estimate, and win most jobs right there on the spot.

Then we would start loading and hauling stuff. It was a boy's dream job, because not only did I get to help, but a lot of the stuff we hauled was not junk at all. Not to me, anyway. Toys, tools, home accessories, games, appliances—even furniture—found their way into the passenger's cab now and then.

Dad seldom negotiated his price and had to be creative with some loads. And he had one big rule—no garbage. We were just not set up for garbage (thank heaven), and we stuck to it, regardless of what a prospect needed. It was my first lesson in business: It's just as important to know what you won't do, as it is to know what you will do.

Dad paid me $5 for every Saturday I worked with him and $2 for every evening. Plus, I got all the hamburgers I could eat and all the pop I could drink. We had an agreement. After every load dumped, we would stop and get a can of pop.

I was the richest kid on the block.

       ❂ ❂ ❂ ❂ ❂ ❂

My first real date was with Sandi Roed. I was a sophomore at Fertile-Beltrami High School, and she was a junior at the neighboring village of Mentor. It was Friday night; I was sixteen, with my newly minted driver's license and ten bucks in my wallet. I picked her up in my dad's new, green 1977 Ford LTD. We went to a drive-in movie, and saw *A Star Is Born*, with Kris Kristofferson and Barbara Streisand. I thought I had truly arrived as an independent, grown-up, all around cool guy. The date was great, Sandi was terrific, but the car was amazing. I wanted to see her again, and soon.

"Not so fast, mister." My dad didn't exactly say it that way, but the outcome was essentially the same.

Father Roger Grundhaus, our parish priest, had been telling me about a program for teenagers called Teens Encounter Christ or TEC for short. I was only mildly interested, because although I was sixteen, I was still a sophomore, and you were supposed to wait until your junior year of high school to go on one of these weekend retreats.

God bless Fr. Roger if he didn't make a few calls on my behalf and got me enrolled early, as in the Saturday morning after my great date with Sandi. My first real date, with a real girl, in a real car—the last thing I wanted to do was to go on a religious retreat the next morning for three days. Forgive me, but I wanted a second date that same weekend.

Saturday morning, my dad had to roust me several times to get ready. Fr. Roger had gone to all this trouble to wrangle me a free pass; it was the least I could do to go and be polite, he chided. "Watch out; if you're not careful, you might actually enjoy it."

I was not a happy camper, nor did I plan to be. I was headed to Park Rapids, Minnesota, to spend the weekend with a bunch of older kids I didn't know, on a retreat I didn't want or need, and I was riding in the backseat of someone else's car, driven by—of all people—a nun, Sister Mary Ann Welsh. (Aren't they all named Mary?)

It would change my life forever.

TEC weekends were created specifically for youth between ages seventeen and twenty-four, designed around personal experiences, not educational dogma. It was all about connecting and involving them on their level, acknowledging that they were very likely to be in transition at this point in their lives, struggling with spirituality, questioning their faith, and wondering whether any of what they'd been taught or had heard about the Catholic church was relevant in their changing world. It was one of the most powerful and impactful programs I have ever been a part of.

In fact, as it turned out, I would end up attending more than twenty TEC weekends—as a leader. My persuasive skills were in full gear by then because more than fifty members of my immediate and extended family eventually attended a retreat. My parents went on to serve on over sixty-five weekend retreats, and later, their help was instrumental in starting the first non-

Catholic TEC program, called Red River Valley TEC, which is still going well to this day.

I guess I was a bit evangelistic before I knew what that was. I even got my favorite priest, Father Ken Opat, O.S.C., to attend a TEC weekend. He ended up becoming the most influential TEC leader in the history of the entire movement. After nearly thirty years, Fr. Ken retired from serving as the Central Minnesota TEC Coordinator, having made a positive, powerful impact on literally tens of thousands of teens and young adults through his ministry and the TEC program.

Talk about impact—within sixty days of attending that first TEC retreat, I made another major decision. I decided to leave home and go to boarding school. I wanted to consider the priesthood, and the best place to do so was at Crosier Seminary Preparatory School run by the Order of the Holy Cross in Onamia, Minnesota, about four hours from Fertile.

The day I moved to Onamia to attend my last two years of high school, my Dad pulled me aside and said he had a gift for me.

Oh, boy! Here it comes. I'll bet he got me a nice stereo system for my room.

Not even close. He handed me a plaque. A plaque? It said: "In all thy ways, acknowledge Him, and He shall direct thy paths. Proverbs 3:6." (KJV)

Gee, great. "Thank you, Dad," I said politely, not realizing then how important that verse would be throughout my career and life.

In the spring of my junior year, after attending for only one semester, I was elected president of the high school. This was unheard of, for a transfer student to come in and beat the leading candidate who had already been there for three years.

As president, I got my own office, and I had a set of master keys for the entire complex. Turns out I wasn't supposed to have those keys, but one of the good Fathers ceremoniously handed me a set anyway and pronounced, "With responsibility comes privilege, Mark." I never forgot that, and never took advantage of the power and privilege that came from holding a high office—not then, not ever.

As president of our student body, I was asked to speak throughout the year, plus I was speaking at the frequent TEC retreats I attended. I never felt more alive than when I was in front of an audience.

If only I could somehow turn this into a career.

Despite the speaking opportunities it would obviously afford, the priesthood was not for me. I liked girls way too much. I didn't put it that way to my spiritual director at Crosier Seminary, a dinosaur of a priest named Father Bill McNiff. I told him that I could better serve God by raising priests and nuns. He did not think that was funny.

My classmates thought it was hilarious.

❀ ❀ ❀ ❀ ❀ ❀

When I graduated, my dad said he had a special gift for me.

A car, I bet he bought me a car. New or used? Geez, don't be greedy, LeBlanc. After all, new or used, it would still be a new car to me.

I put on my game face as I opened the small package. It wasn't a box, and it wasn't lumpy.

The keys must be in the ignition. I bet there's a pink slip in here.

Again, not even close. It was a book. A small, $2.99 paperback by some guy with a name that looked like a giant typo and sounded like a cartoon character: Og Mandino. My dad gave me a copy of *The Greatest Salesman in the World.* It was Dad's favorite book, having received it as a gift from a priest who admired my dad's entrepreneurial spirit and obvious sales talent. In fact, Dad loved that book so much he actually bought a case of them and handed them out as gifts to his friends—and apparently—as a high school graduation gift to his very own son.

The book is an inspirational and motivational parable about a man who changed his life, became successful and wealthy from the priceless wisdom of ten ancient scrolls handed down for thousands of years to one, chosen recipient. I'm not spoiling anything for those of you who haven't read the book by telling you that the story line is about how this one man finds the next chosen recipient, whose charge it will be to tell the world about the scrolls and how to use them to live a better life.

It's the kind of book you can read in one sitting, and I did, mostly to please my dad. Then I read it again. I decided to read it daily, just as it was prescribed in the first of the ten scrolls. One scroll, three times a day for thirty days before going on to the next scroll. I spent the next ten months reading the assigned scroll, immersing myself in its principles. Unbeknownst to me at the time, it would influence my thinking, frame my actions (and reactions), and fuel my spirit for the rest of my life.

THE CAMINO

One More Step

I don't know how long I sat on that bench after walking only two stinking miles. Did I mention the rain? It seemed that every excuse I had ever come up with for not reaching my goals flooded my mind.

That little town I had just come from was inviting, and only two miles back the other way, downhill. What if I could take a bus from there to Barcelona and just hang out for five weeks? This Camino thing was a dumb idea to begin with.

The Camino is short for the Camino de Santiago, one of the three great pilgrimages of the world, with Rome and Jerusalem being the other two. In 2006, I had never heard of it. In fact, the first time it was mentioned to me, at my brother, John's, dining room table by his friend Jim Hingeley, it had come up in conversation as "Jim's little walk in Spain." As I listened to Jim explain his little five-hundred-mile trek across Northern Spain, I was captivated.

The most popular route of the pilgrimage starts in Southern France and ends in Northwestern Spain, at the Cathedral of Santiago de Compostela, where the remains of St. James, one of Christ's twelve Apostles, are buried. So, Jim's little walk was not such a bad nickname, after all, because Camino de Santiago means "The Way of St. James" in English. St. James' remains were discovered there in the ninth century, and in the eleventh century, people began walking to Santiago from all over Europe, believing the pilgrimage would wipe away all of a person's sins.

Today an average of one hundred people from all over the world, of all faiths, and for many reasons, both personal and spiritual, begin the walk every single day of the year. The record was set in 2004, when 179,994 people made the amazing journey.

Jim's story gnawed at me every day for weeks, until I finally made the decision to go for that same little five-hundred-mile walk. I looked ahead on my calendar and the soonest I could carve out forty days in a row would be two years later. So, on that decisive day in December 2006, I inked "Camino" on my calendar and colored myself "gone" September 7–October 13, 2008.

I am not sure I believed that my sins would be wiped away. That was probably just another one of our Catholic things. I did, however, think that simply walking, eating, sleeping, and, yes, praying, for thirty days in a foreign country—all alone—might be a relief and welcome respite coming just after what I knew would be a whirlwind of highs and lows in my personal life and professional career. And truth be told, of course, I had a few sins to get rid of too.

@ @ @ @ @ @

When I ran out of excuses and got tired of hearing myself whine on that bench, I decided that this was one mountain that could wait until tomorrow to be climbed, what with the late start and all. Besides, I realized I could call it a day in just a few more kilometers, at the first *refugio* (aka hostel) I spotted on the map. I hoisted myself off the bench and discarded a few of my own items that I suddenly deemed too heavy to lug around for a month.

That night, over dinner with other walkers, I asked a woman from England about her experience. (I couldn't speak a word of any other language, so God bless the U.K.) She and two other friends were walking the Camino in stages at the rate of one week a year for five years. This was year three. She didn't appear to be in very good shape, and was, in fact, a little overweight. OK. I'm a guy, and I was trying to be polite just then. Her name was Judith, and she was heavy. There I was, a guy who had walked five miles at 5:00 a.m. every single day for sixty days to get in shape for this hike, and I was dying after a few uphill miles.

How in the heck had she managed a week of this, two years in a row?

Aloud, I phrased my question quite differently and simply asked if she had any advice for me.

"Mark, you can always take another step. No matter how tired you are, no matter how miserable you are, you can always take another step," Judith said.

At that moment, her words were more inspiring than all ten Og Mandino scrolls combined, and more useful than anything I could dredge from the database of motivational quotes I had stored somewhere in my brain. I thanked God for her every day on the Camino.

The next day, I began the ascent of Mount Leopeder, and it was painful. Other walkers would pass me, and it seemed as if they actually felt sorry for me. What message was I sending with my demeanor? I practically chanted Judith's advice: "You can always take another step."

Then I began counting my steps in lots of one hundred. True! I'd count a hundred steps, pause, and take ten breaths. Then another hundred steps, pause, and take ten breaths. Repeat. Repeat. Repeat. All day. All the way up that mountain.

I reached the top at about 4:00 p.m., took off my hiking shoes, peeled off my socks, and lay on the ground. I wanted to cry. As other walkers came up the trail, paused only briefly, and then started their descent, it dawned on me. *Refugios* can fill up fast, leaving you no place to sleep, and no choice but to wander. I had better get going. At least it was all downhill now.

I know, I know. They say downhill is worse than uphill. They are correct. The impact on my knees and hips was excruciating. All I could do was my best attempt at one baby step after another, all the way down into the village of Roncevalles. I hobbled into a *refugio* that was a converted monastery and quickly registered for the night. I knew enough not to expect my own room or even something as cozy as four, six, or eight to a room. I will admit, though, that I was a little wide-eyed with wonder to see sixty bunk beds in one room, which, when I did the math, meant 120 people in one room overnight. Let me share with you that 120 people, ages twenty to seventy in one room overnight is a symphony of sounds you cannot imagine unless you have been there.

It was the best five bucks I ever spent.

CHAPTER TWO

That's Life

I'm no Frank Sinatra, but I have been a printer, a broker, a pizza guy, a paste-up artist, Pac Man king. I've been up the creek, down in the dumps, over the moon, flat on my back, and out and out broke. Not necessarily in that order.

The only thing I had in common with most other eighteen to twenty-two-year-olds during this four-year, post high school period was that we were all trying to find ourselves. Whereas they were looking in college classrooms (not to mention a few frat houses and dorm rooms), I was not. I was all over the map, in both the geographic and metaphorical sense of the phrase.

I knew I didn't want to be a priest, and I knew that for sure. So, why not try real estate right after graduation? I tried it in Colorado, living with an uncle while pining for a nurse I was crazy about in St. Cloud, Minnesota. No, real estate was not my thing either. I came home to work in a clothing store in

Crookston, Minnesota, pay off some debt, and save enough money to enroll in college and move to St. Cloud. Which I did, and was promptly dumped by the nurse. My college try was not one of those from which the cliché evolved. I lasted a semester and a half, but did manage to find my forte after hours and hours of study, perspiration, and practice—Pac Man.

Stop laughing. I got paid. I became a manager at the arcade, and then helped the owner start three more family video centers, which led to my hiring a guy named Bill Nelson to manage one of them. Bill became my first consulting client, although at the time, neither one of us knew that's what I was doing, nor that's what you called it. I was into Pac Man and knew something about starting and running a business, albeit a video arcade. Bill was into karate and wanted to open a karate school. I don't remember the advice I gave him, and neither does Bill, but it must have been useful because today Bill is a seventh degree black belt, an author, and his karate school is still thriving in its original location.

Bill and I became fast friends, as close to being brothers as you can get without being adopted. (Although Bill's mom, Priscilla "Tootie" Nelson, would have told you the only thing missing was the paperwork.) Tootie was always there for Bill and her other boys, young men like me who were struggling and stumbling along that rocky path to find our way in the world. Turns out that Tootie was an Og Mandino fan, too, and she was impressed with the fact that I had spent ten months reading the *Greatest Salesman* scrolls.

"Mark, what do you want to do with your life?" she asked me at what felt like point blank range.

We were having lunch, and I don't remember my exact answer. Something about using my voice, perhaps broadcasting. . . I don't know. . . I used to speak a lot in my TEC days, that was fun.

Tootie's best friend was Joan Kennedy, who happened to be quite an accomplished motivational speaker. What a coincidence! Tootie made it her mission to introduce us and called her that same afternoon.

Joan invited me to attend the December 1982 meeting of the Minnesota Chapter of the National Speakers Association (NSA). I was twenty-one years old in a room full of effusive, animated, and articulate grownups who were overly dressed for success and seemed to prefer the bear hug over the handshake as the preferred method of welcoming a newcomer. When the program began, I was transfixed by the speakers. Even the announcements were interesting. It brought back memories, flashbacks to my TEC days, to that glorious feeling of truly being alive, being in front of an audience, making a difference, wishing there was a way I could make a living that way. I thought the only way to do that involved becoming a priest and delivering a weekly sermon. Oh, happy day! I was hooked.

⊗　⊗　⊗　⊗　⊗　⊗

I've always loved my family and being with them, even at age twenty-one and especially during the holidays. I never had to go home for a visit; I always wanted to go. This year, still energized by my recent NSA experience, I went home for Christmas as usual, and left with a lot more than new shirts and socks.

It was pretty much the typical holiday for us. We gathered with friends and family. We ate and ate and drank. We watched football, played games, and fell asleep off and on, sometimes while sitting, sometimes stretched out on the couch. Eventually, my dad and I were the last ones in the living room, and we got to talking. Dad had been thinking, he said, which usually meant there was another entrepreneurial idea he needed to hear out loud for himself in order to judge its merits. Wrong, not this time.

"You know what I noticed tonight, Mark?" I could tell that Dad was about to become philosophical and rhetorical, so all I had to do was raise my head off the back of the couch, open my eyes, and mumble a "Hmmm, what?" in his direction.

"I watched everyone at the table tonight. We always put too much food on our plate, and we always take servings of things we don't really want. Instead of doubling up on the things we really want, everybody takes a dab of this, a little bit of everything. Just to be polite, I suppose, which is nice for Grandma, your mom, and Aunt Jane or Georgia, but it doesn't make sense," he said, staring at the ceiling from his Lazy Boy.

He pushed the handle on the side of the chair to sit upright and looked over at me. Thank goodness my eyes were open.

"Think about it. Why do we do that? We put too much on our plates, yet never get enough of what we really want."

I paused, getting the sense that he wasn't really talking about food. I sat up on the couch, leaned forward in his direction.

"I know what I really want. Dad, in fact, I know what I want to do with the rest of my life," I ventured. "I want to be a professional speaker."

Dad shook his head slightly in an effort to clear his thoughts.

"A professional speaker? Can you make any money doing that?"

"I don't know, Dad, but I went to this meeting of the Minnesota Speakers Association, and all of the people there are rich."

⊙ ⊙ ⊙ ⊙ ⊙ ⊙

Og Mandino's little book was paying off that winter. I had left the video arcade and was barely paying my bills as a straight commission salesman working for a printing company. Becoming a professional speaker was my destination, and I could see it clearly. Printing sales was the vehicle to get me there.

Until I was rear-ended. Literally. The frazzled mom was refereeing a squabble between her kids in the back seat, didn't see my brake lights, and slammed on her own brakes a little too late. It was not a major accident, but it did cause serious injury. It put me in plenty of pain, kept me in and out of physical therapy, and landed me in the hospital for a major back operation three years later. Two important things happened during my recovery period.

One, I met the woman I would marry. She worked at the printing company I represented, and during my convalescence, she visited and even gave me a get-well gift. It was a T-square, and she taught me how to spec type and do simple paste-up and key lining. These are ancient terms in our electronic world today, but for me, before even the days of desktop publishing, they were the tools that unlocked a world of possibilities and gave me the freedom to think beyond the boundaries of selling other people's goods and services. Why not sell my own services?

Two, I also made a decision. I decided then and there at the age of twenty-two, that I never again wanted to have a boss. I would live or die on my own and do whatever it took to make it work. I would starve if I had to, and I nearly did.

First step, I decided, was to join that speaker group. Imagine my surprise when I received my information packet from the headquarters of the National Speakers Association, and there, on the board of directors list was a name I knew well, Og Mandino. *He's alive?!*

I was young, out of work, out of money, but nothing, and I mean nothing, would stop me from going to the NSA national convention being held in San Francisco in the summer of 1983. I had a tangible destination in sight. I also had my new-found commitment to being my own boss, and I knew how I would do it. Instead of working for one printer on straight commission and letting them keep the profit, I would become a print broker, shop a stable of suppliers, buy wholesale, mark it up, and keep 100 percent of the profit myself.

Brilliant! That's how one person described my business plan when I bravely shared it, seeking objective feedback as she cut my hair. Her name was Arlene Teigen, my hairdresser. (I called her The Lady Who Cut My Hair back then.) She encouraged me to talk to her husband, Tom, about the idea. Tom Teigen was a loan officer at Security Federal Bank.

He didn't call my plan brilliant, per se, but he believed in me enough to give me a $3,000 loan. My payment was $82.64 a month and it would take me forty-eight months to pay it off. I put the $3,000 to immediate use in launching my business. First, I caught up on my rent. Then I bought, in this order, groceries, a new suit, a reservation for the National Speakers Association convention, and an airplane ticket to San Francisco.

Back pain? Excruciating on a three-hour flight. Worth it? You bet. I not only saw Og Mandino; I met him. We had a conversation. He let me take his picture, and he let someone else take our picture together. I was overwhelmed and energized at the same time from meeting Og, by the speakers I heard, by the generosity of the members who shared their experience and tips, by the volume of information I absorbed like a sponge.

When I returned home, I was organizing my membership materials and notes from the conference, and I came across a postcard from Lee Boyan, the 1983 president of the NSA Minnesota chapter. It included a simple, handwritten P.S.—"Mark, the world needs to hear you."

I was now a man with a mission.

Here's the thing about being on a mission. You're either focused on it like a laser beam, or, well, you're not. If you're not, you're probably distracted, going off in all kinds of well-intended directions, thinking, "Hey, I could do that! And that. Oh, and look at that over there—look at how much money that person is making." Tangents disguised as opportunities—that's what I call them today.

Back then, as a newly minted small business owner, my tangents were more about survival. You see, I had picked up a number of creative and printing clients, but not enough to support me in the style to which I had become accustomed—a rented basement room from my cousin Karen and her husband, Dick, in a sleepy suburb of St. Paul. And let's not forget the always-looming $82.64 monthly payment on my business loan.

I needed something to tide me over until my revenues would support me, as well as my dream to speak.

I found the perfect thing—pizza. No, it wasn't comfort food. It was pizza delivery. I could do that! I could deliver pizzas on Thursday, Friday, and Saturday nights and make enough to support myself. Small business owner by day, pizza man by night. It was a humbling experience, but one I look back on with a measure of pride. Because despite the good tips and the temptation to expand my hours, I didn't let it become a distraction for me. I knew what I wanted more than anything else, and pizza delivery was a means to a greater end, the first spoke in the wheel that would become my whatever-it-takes attitude toward building my business, and eventually toward helping others build theirs.

۞ ۞ ۞ ۞ ۞ ۞

If there was any distraction at that time—and perhaps distraction is not the right word—it was that I was essentially trying to launch two businesses at the same time. I wanted more than anything to be speaking, and given my creative and printing resources, I was able to create some pretty slick-looking tools to promote myself. Didn't know what to do with them, mind you, but boy, did they look good.

And then I got the call. My first paid speaking engagement. From a speakers bureau, no less. If you are not familiar with the speaking industry, a bureau is akin to a talent agency. They work with clients, many of them big name corporations who are looking for just the right speaker for an event. The bureau recommends one of its speakers, handles the booking as well as the billing, pays the speaker, and keeps a commission. This bureau's client was Arby's, as in roast beef, the fast food franchisor, and they were looking for a "young motivational speaker who could fire up the younger managers and assistant managers" at an evening meeting in Minneapolis.

I can do that! The fee was $300, and believe me, in 1985, I was ecstatic.

I was, of course, nervous about the presentation, but prepared as best I could, given the fact that I didn't really have a subject to go on beyond motivate young managers, and I didn't have a standard speech or so-called signature story to fall back on. So I reminded myself of my TEC days, my twenty-plus weekends of inspiring young people. I probably threw in some material from *The Greatest Salesman*, and God only knows what else. I wore the same suit I had bought to go to the National Speakers Association conference, and delivered the program lookin' good and feelin' pretty smart.

After the meeting, I met my close friend, John Givogre, D.C., to celebrate over a drink, and I told him it went well, maybe not great, but certainly I was on my way to living my dream. Not only had I been discovered, but, man, oh, man, I had arrived.

I told him all about the speakers bureau and how the agent who booked me was excited to have found someone like me he could take to other franchisors. Visions of multiple bookings, more fees, and all the roast beef sandwiches I could eat danced in my head. We toasted my big break—and so early in my career.

"Have you called your dad yet? He's going to be so excited for you," John said.

"No, not yet. I will, but my dad might not see it the way I do. He comes from a different era and doesn't really understand the whole speaking thing."

"What's not to understand?" John asked.

"Well, it's just that I remember my dad saying he hoped I didn't become successful too quickly, something about his having seen too many people close a big deal or get a giant commission early on in their career and then they stopped working, took their foot off the gas pedal, just coasted, and never really got up to speed again," I explained.

We both agreed that my dad wasn't talking about me; it was probably good advice for someone else, but not for me.

Then the letter came. Oh, boy! My first check.

What? This can't be right. The check wasn't for the full amount we had agreed on. Then I read the letter. Al Porte from Speakers USA, the agent who I thought was going to put me on tour, sent me the client's evaluation of my presentation. Apparently they were hugely disappointed in the younger motivational speaker and didn't think he was all that motivating to begin with. In fact, they made some remark about my being de-motivating, and refused to pay the balance of the fee. In the envelope was my net share of the original $150 deposit, minus the agent's 25 percent commission. The check was for the sum total of $112.50.

I bombed in my first paid professional speech. I didn't give another one for three years.

THE CAMINO

Learn One Thing

When I left for Spain, so many people asked me why I was going, was there something in particular I was searching for, hoping to solve, working on, or working through? No, not really. I didn't have a good answer, but the one I probably gave most often was to quote what others had told me would happen as a result of the Camino, whether I went there seeking it or not. "Everyone who goes will learn one thing, be reminded of one thing, and let go of one thing."

It was only Day Three of my Camino, so I wasn't expecting anything profound. I did figure out right away that there is no lollygagging in a *refugio*. The lights come on at 6:00 a.m., and you've got exactly two hours to get up, get fed, and get out. No sleeping in, no layover days allowed. They need the day to clean and make ready for the next wave of walkers who arrive each afternoon. This is the rule and the regimen of the *refugio*, repeated 365 days a year across Northern Spain. No exceptions. No kidding.

I was up and out in plenty of time that morning, thankful to have no blisters (yet). But that was the only positive point I scored on my physical fitness self-assessment. Elsewhere, everywhere, something on my body ached, screamed, and/or winced with every step, at all times, despite the terrain being relatively level with only a few gradual inclines and descents here and there. So, who would have guessed that with plenty of pain to occupy my thoughts, this would be the day I'd learn my greatest insight. Certainly not I.

Don't ask me how or why, but I found myself thinking about numbers. OK, perhaps it was sparked by my miserable thought that if this were only Day Three, how in the world was I going to survive it, let alone another thirty. Thirty days. I read one of those ten scrolls three times a day for thirty days. That's ninety readings per month times ten scrolls equals nine hundred impressions, my mind's calculator told me, using my printer's lingo from the past.

Every thirty days. "Your success lies in the phrase 'every thirty days.'" How many times had I said that in my presentations and to my coaching clients? A gazillion, give or take a million.

Numbers. I ask my coaching clients to "send me their numbers." How often? Every thirty days. I have them create an Optimistic Number, that number that "represents the amount of work you want to do at your current fee level with your fun meter on max and having the kind of balance you want between home and work." How often? Every thirty days. Once they have an Optimistic Number, I tell them that the key to being at or near that Optimistic Number (every thirty days) is for them to do three High Value Activites (HVAs), which must also be framed by a number. As in, "make three phone calls, mail ten postcards, spend thirty minutes writing a blog post." More numbers.

What was it with me and numbers? And then I remembered, it wasn't that I was into numbers as much as I was into measurement. Anything worth doing is worth measuring. Benchmarks. That's what my numbers were—are—really all about. Benchmarks, not goals. Benchmarks might be a kissing cousin to goals, but they're not the same. Benchmarks measure an activity or an outcome.

Your goal might be, "More balance between work and home." OK, then how many date nights will you create—you guessed it—every thirty days? Want to lose weight? How many times will you exercise, go to yoga, play tennis, take a walk, attend Weight Watchers—whatever—every thirty days? Want to sell more products or services? How many networking meetings will you attend, phone calls will you make, emails will you send—every, well, you know?

There I was, on a walk that many would consider spiritual in nature, and instead of praying or counting my blessings, or even counting my steps that day, there I was reviewing my own numbers, my own benchmarks, asking myself the proverbial question I ask my clients:

What do you want more of?

I rattled off my own answers quickly. Less debt, new clients, more speaking engagements. Financial benchmarks, sales benchmarks, marketing benchmarks. Easy. *What else?* More fun, less weight, more energy. Piece of cake. Well, not literally, of course, but creating benchmarks for dancing, entertaining, and exercising was a cinch.

Richer relationships. What? Where did that come from? Not my head, nor even my heart. It seemed to come from my soul. I walked and limped and walked and tried to go back to the easy stuff. But as I poured over my life and life's work, my thoughts wandered to the hundreds, if not thousands, of people that had come and gone.

And then there were more questions. Why had I taken so many so seriously? Why had I cared what people I barely knew thought of me? Why did I work so hard to impress so few?

And sure enough, the answer, in the form of yet another question, became clear to me once I began to frame it with numbers. It seemed as if I had one thousand friends. However, truth be told, they were more like connections, acquaintances, or attendees. I might have one hundred friends. A couple dozen good friends and maybe ten or so close friends.

Right in the middle of my cataloguing and classifying, the question of all questions, the only question that really matters in this world, came crashing into my consciousness:

Who do you love, and who loves you?

Instantly the faces of a mere handful of people outside my family came to mind. They cared about me unconditionally. They cared about who I was, not what I had done or accomplished or could do for them. I remembered reading somewhere that if you have two or three people who love you unconditionally, without judgment, then you are a rich person. In my mind's eye, I saw the faces of each of those five individuals, my "Fab Five," if you will.

And in that moment, I learned my one thing: I am a very rich man.

CHAPTER THREE

On the Press

Cousin Karen and her husband, Dick, my above-ground landlords, had no idea I was delivering pizzas at night, although they did come up with some scintillating conjecture one night as to why I was leaving and what I was doing until two in the morning those days (and nights). They also had no idea I had spoken to, or bombed in front of, all those young managers at Arby's. All they knew was that I had set up shop in their basement using the T-square that my eventual bride-to-be had given me. Then, with the profit I made on a relatively large project, I bought my first stand-alone, single-purpose piece of office furniture—a drawing table for $169.95. Up until then I made the best of my bed, dresser, and floor to do my paste-up voodoo. I said no to the frivolous $40 optional side attachment for organizing my drafting instruments, border tape, knives, wax, and other tools of the trade. I could leave all that stuff on the floor.

❀　❀　❀　❀　❀　❀

My car accident on June 9, 1983, not only impacted my decision
to start my own business, it helped me grow it by introducing
me to my first, honest-to-goodness consulting client. In addition
to the medical doctors who treated me, I also sought chiropractic care from Joe McKiernan, D.C. in Sauk Rapids. I was his
patient, to be sure, but eventually we became friends as well.
As Dr. Joe learned more about me and my business, we began
to chat about his practice and the other two chiropractic clinics
he owned. When I moved away to St. Paul, he referred me to
another chiropractor nearby, but he would still call me from time
to time and invite me back up to the St. Cloud area for lunch
and maybe some creative brainstorming around ways to grow his
clinic. A lot of my friends still lived up there, so I could always
rationalize making the three-hour, round-trip drive. Besides, it
was a great ego boost, affirming, and validating to spend time
with someone who put his faith in me and believed in my work.

Until he asked me one too many questions. It felt as if we
had crossed the line from friendship to business. He certainly
did not do anything wrong, nor did he have any intentions of
taking advantage of me. I was the one who undervalued my
talent and failed to manage his expectations.

One night, while delivering pizzas, I got to thinking about all
those drives to St. Cloud, and I decided I was going to propose

NEVER *be the* SAME

a monthly contract to Dr. Joe. (I had never heard of the term retainer.) When I finished my route at 2:00 a.m., I pulled a piece of paper from my piling system on the floor and crafted a simple letter that included two options for a six-month agreement. One was for $200 per month and one was for $400 per month. I put the proposal in an envelope, and the next day I put it in the mail. I was scared to death and was certain it would be the end of our friendship, with no hope for any other kind of relationship. When I did not hear from him for three weeks, I knew it was over.

Then, after another night of pizza delivery into the wee hours of the morning, I returned to my basement/office/bedroom to see the red blinking light on my answering machine, signaling that a message was waiting for me.

"Mark, Joe McKiernan here. I just wanted to let you know I am signing your agreement for $400 and putting a check in the mail for the first two months. Looking forward to working with you. We'll talk soon."

What? Did I hear that correctly? It was good thing I had parked the whole professional speaker idea, because I was rendered speechless. Giddy, but speechless. When the check arrived a few days later, I felt rich—it would take nearly fifty hours delivering pizzas to make $400, and there I was with a check for $800, with four additional months of $400 I could count on. I dared to imagine that the light at the end of the pizza delivery tunnel might soon be coming from my taillights as I left that job behind.

Best of all, I didn't bomb. In fact, our first big promotion brought in more than twenty new patients. I was still measuring success by the fact that my checks didn't bounce, but in the chiropractic circles that Dr. Joe circulated, twenty patients was worth bragging about, and he did. The good Dr. Joe told his pals about our success, and my phone started to ring. Within a year I had four more retainers, and those eventually connected me to the Minnesota Chiropractic Association, the Midwest Chiropractic Consultants, the International Association of Chiropractic Industrial Consultants, and scores of individual chiropractors. And then the dentists began to call, and then independent professionals of all types.

I was twenty-four years old when I hung up my pizza delivery hat. Oh, happy day. Who said you couldn't be living your dream from a basement? At least a big part of your dream, anyway.

◦ ◦ ◦ ◦ ◦ ◦

SPEAKER UPDATE:

I know I said that I retreated like a frightened turtle over the whole Arby's debacle, and I did. But I did come out of my shell just long enough, and enough times, to stay connected and active in the Minnesota Chapter of the National Speakers

Association. In fact, I attended every meeting and was the first one to volunteer for anything. I was happy to meet with any professional speaker, at any time, for any reason. Whether they were successful or not, I had to surround myself with people in the profession. Meanwhile, I was gung ho to grow my business. Hmm, I liked the sound of that.

⊚ ⊚ ⊚ ⊚ ⊚ ⊚

In the 1967 movie *The Graduate*, Dustin Hoffman's character was given a one-word piece of advice about securing his future: plastics. Twenty-some-odd years later, my word was Apple. As in computers. Before the words "desktop publishing" could even be coined, I invested $2,500 in a Macintosh 512, the second in Apple's long line of computers. It was nicknamed the Fat Mac because its 512K built-in memory was quadruple that of the first Macintosh, and it came with MacPaint and MacWrite. These were two software programs that made my T-square and drawing table virtually obsolete. I invested another $7,000 in one of Apple's first laser printers and was no longer locked into brokering the smaller print jobs and marking them up for resale to my clients. Poof—I was in the printing business, and it began to grow.

Oh! I got married in 1985 to Jill, the girlfriend who gave me my first T-square.

The desktop publishing side of my business enabled me to sell even more services, and my $9,500 investment paid for itself in six months. I still had to buy out larger print projects, so when I got wind that a local printer was going to shut down and liquidate his equipment, I jumped on the opportunity. I called my close friend Dr. John, the same one who celebrated my first paid speech, and who was, in fact, the Mendota Heights chiropractor Dr. Joe referred me to when I set up shop in Cousin Karen's basement. In a moment disguised as business acumen, Dr. John loaned me $30,000 to buy the printing business. I know now that it was really a moment of magnanimous generosity on his part, and he later told me that he never really expected to get his money back (and he almost didn't, several times).

Now I had overhead and mouths to feed—employees! I worked morning, noon, and night, and about forty-five Saturdays a year for the next five years. Interestingly enough, to me at least, I saw myself as a creative/graphics/printing guy. Yet my growing base of clients saw me as someone who could make a difference in their business. Even in their speaking business. Turns out my pals at NSA wanted to hear more about ways to make their brochures and marketing tools more interesting and attention getting. What if they couldn't afford printing—what could they do then to grow their business? I had ideas, and they wanted to hear those, too. If they wanted to hear what I had to say, perhaps other business owners, other groups of business owners would be interested, too?

They were! And my evaluations were getting better. Let me rephrase that, because anything would be deemed better than bombing. My evaluations were good. Good enough that some people in my audience approached me afterward and wanted to work with me. That was how it was supposed to work, but it was still new to me; in fact, it was a bit of a surprise. Not to Mike McKinley, an accomplished speaker, and member of the NSA Minnesota chapter.

"Of course your evaluations are getting better," he said. "You've weathered the ups and downs of having your own business for ten years. How many thirty-one-year-olds have done that? It's called credibility. You're a walking, talking small business success story."

That did it. I decided to sell my business (which I did, in May of 1992) and start my own speaking business (which I did, in September of 1992). I called it Small Business Success. Brilliant!

And I didn't earn a nickel for a year.

Be Reminded

Whoever came up with that "learn one thing, be reminded of one thing, and let go of one thing" greatly underestimated the "be reminded" part of the prophecy. Be reminded of one thing? Are you kidding? When you only have you to occupy your thoughts day after day, mile after mile, step by step, you're going to remember a lot, and I, for one, was reminded of more than one thing.

There were physical reminders. Blisters, for instance, reminded me that no matter how much you pay for your shoes (or for your socks), no matter how many miles you walked every day before Spain, there is no way to prepare yourself for the actual use and abuse you're going to inflict on your feet once you get there.

I awoke one morning in a *refugio*, still half asleep, dreaming of a better place, and not quite sure of where I was. As I came out of my sleepy haze, I stretched my body and wiggled my toes. The shocking pain traveled through my body as if I'd been zapped by a taser gun. What the—? Who the—? How the—?

Blisters. When did those happen?

I swung my legs over the side of the cot and gingerly touched my feet to the floor. The next wave of pain was even worse. I looked at an octogenarian on the next cot over. He bid me, "Good morning," and I wanted to suggest there was nothing good about this morning. Instead, we exchanged pleasantries, which instantly reminded me that I had a whopping fifteen miles to walk on those bad boys that day.

When you are walking on blistered feet, the worst steps are about the first hundred or so. Then you get into a rhythm and the pain seems almost manageable, unless you stop to rest. When you start again, the searing pain returns tenfold, for another hundred steps or so, and ups the ante until the next stop. I learned this lesson quickly and learned that you can tell who else has blisters and who does not on the Camino. The blistered walk like the living dead. They limp, stumble, wince, and stop. They look to others for sympathy, but to no avail. You have your own pain to deal with.

As I was contemplating whether or not to risk a rest stop, I heard myself wallowing in self-pity. Bleeding blisters and so many miles to go. Thirty pounds in my backpack. Poor little me. No one knew my pain.

Grow up, LeBlanc.

When you only have you to occupy your thoughts, you also hear voices. And this one came with visuals. In my mind's eye, I saw soldiers, uniforms, and weapons. I thought of all the men and women in the armed services and hung my head. I had a cot and pillow every night and never had to sleep in the rain or snow. I didn't have to carry a gun with real bullets. Better yet, no one was shooting at me. Men and women in the military often carry more than fifty pounds on their backs. The only extra weight I carried that day was a ham and cheese sandwich.

Now, whenever I see a veteran or person on active duty, I am reminded of my blisters. Yes, they brought some measure of pain, along with a fresh perspective on what it means to serve our country. They remind me to tell that person "thank you" whenever I can, and I do.

❀ ❀ ❀ ❀ ❀ ❀

In her book, *Walk in a Relaxed Manner*, Joyce Rupp recounts her experiences on the Camino in vivid detail. I read her book almost a year before traveling to Spain and found her experience enlightening, daunting, and frightening.

She warned her readers that if you walked the Camino, you might experience exactly what it's like to be homeless, to live and walk as a homeless person—and be treated as such. I pretty much figured on the first part happening because it was true; I would not have a guaranteed reservation, a rock solid assurance that I would have a place to stay every night so, yes, I'd be on a daily search for a place to lay my head, just as a homeless person must.

But to be treated as a homeless person? I was an American tourist and it was obvious. No way. But I was way wrong.

※ ※ ※ ※ ※ ※

I started my Camino with one pair of trekking pants. I paid a decent price for them, and I figured they would certainly last thirty days. About a week or so into it, my trekking pants exploded. Yes, exploded is the right word. They did not tear or rip; the fabric just fell apart. And not in the leg region. The seat of my pants had somehow disintegrated right before my eyes. Well, not *my* eyes, actually, but certainly before those belonging to anyone walking behind me.

I was at least two days away from a city large enough to have a retail store that sold pants of any kind, let alone pants that would last me another three weeks of wear (and not tear) on the trail. I prayed that walkers behind me had their eyes on the trail, not on my ass.

Two days later I walked into the city of Astorga and found a sporting goods store. My days of southern exposure were near their end. (Pun intended.) See? I was already on my way to finding the humor in the whole scene, figuring it would be great for a few laughs and would make great material in a speech some day.

The sporting goods store was fairly large and modern, with four twenty-something sales clerks stocking shelves, tidying up the store, going about whatever the manager had instructed them to do when no customers were present. I waited at the front counter for help, not knowing where to begin my search for a new pair of pants. No one was working the counter at the time, so I managed to get eye contact with each of the floor clerks when they glanced my way, yet no one came forth. Perhaps they were assigned a territory?

I waited patiently and still no one came. I began to wonder if it was a cultural thing. Did no one want to make a sale today? My Visa card was visible from fifty paces, of that I was certain.

Finally, a young woman who was most likely the store manager approached me and said something in Spanish. I had no clue what she had said, and thank heaven she couldn't hear the voice inside my head.

Come on, surely someone speaks English. Don't all the little kids learn English here in Spain? Isn't it mandatory? How do they ever expect to make it in this world if they don't know how to read, write, and speak my native tongue? How hard can this be? All I want is a pair of pants for God's sake.

Time for Plan B. Gesturing. I pointed at my pants and directed her attention to the affected area. She chuckled her understanding and motioned me off in the general direction of the men's section. She did not accompany me the way they do in the grocery store at home. I heard muffled laughter from the clerks on the other side of the store, but didn't really care at that point. Heck, this was eventually supposed to be a funny story, right?

I could not find a pair of pants in my size and called for the manager to come back over. I saw her wince ever so slightly and glance at her colleagues before hesitantly walking towards me. It was as if she'd lost a bet or drawn the short straw.

I hadn't shaved in about ten days, nor checked a mirror that morning. I knew I didn't look or feel my best, and I was tired, but not repelling. And then it hit me, right between the eyes— literally in my nose. I reeked. And so did my backpack. Even though I showered daily (well, almost) and washed my clothes as often as I could, I never could completely rid myself of the toxic smell that permeates your every pore after all those days of walking. I looked and smelled like a homeless person. I was in a foreign country, and no one understood a word I was saying. Or cared.

Wanting to make this as painless as possible for both of us, I did my best to gesture and find out if there were any pants in the back room or at any other stores. Nothing. Apparently, no sale was worth having to serve me. I hung my head in shame and left the store.

I didn't have the courage to find another store or ask another soul for assistance. In fact, I walked three more days wearing my shredded pants before I finally found a store in Leon, where a very kind someone saw past my appearance and reached out to help—without having seen my Visa, by the way. I bought two pair of trekking pants, the kind with the zip-off pants legs so that you get a pair of shorts out of the deal, too. I threw in a pair of gloves for the nippy mornings, as well, and hoped that my kind someone salesperson was working on commission.

Now, whenever I see a homeless person, I am reminded of what it feels like to be *treated* as a homeless person, to be invisible, pre-judged, and rejected. I know it's unrealistic to financially help every person who stretches out a hand, and I'm not suggesting you do. But perhaps you can look past that immediate impression and all the assumptions that typically come with it. Perhaps you can pick your moments, go with your gut, and make that homeless person's day just a little better. It won't take much, and it's hard to put a price on letting people know they matter to someone. Someone like you.

⚬ ⚬ ⚬ ⚬ ⚬ ⚬

I was reminded of regrets. Hurts, losses, mistakes, disappointments, and a fair amount of anger and resentment showed up, too. Problems, both personal and professional—my divorce from Jill after nineteen years of marriage—they all replayed in my mind one day, as if I were watching a movie, a montage of all the things that were painful, caused others pain, or somehow went wrong in my life. Just as I was really getting worked up, blaming this person, that situation, including God and the Camino itself, I was reminded of one very important fact.

I was the star of this movie. I was in every scene. Every challenge, issue, or obstacle had a common denominator—me. Could it be that my attitude, ignorance, approach, or arrogance had played a role in the way a certain scene or struggle played out? Of course it did. More than a reminder, this was a revelation. The only thing missing was the musical score, darkened sky, and a bolt of lightening to strike the trail and stop me in my tracks.

Never again would I point my finger at someone else for my hurt, failures, or sadness. I vowed that I would accept 100 percent responsibility for all areas of my life, no matter what or who was involved. And you know, by the end of the day, my pack, my step, and my heart felt lighter. Wait! Letting go of blame—perhaps this wasn't one of the things I was reminded of. Perhaps this was the one thing I was to let go of as a result of my Camino?

No. I wouldn't discover that one until the very last day, when I arrived in front of the Cathedral of Santiago. Darn that Saint James.

CHAPTER FOUR

My Defining Moment

September is back-to-school for some folks. For me it was back-to-business. Back to launching my dream, my speaking business. I thought I was being productive. I wrote a few letters, met for lunch with former clients, went to networking meetings. I felt busy, but learned that there's a difference between productivity—checking things off a To-Do list—and progress. Progress would have moved me closer to my dream of being a full-time professional (paid) speaker. I had lots of check marks next to my To-Do items, but no checks. No one seemed to want or need anything I had to offer, and I longed for the days of solving problems with my three hundred printing clients and having fifty vendors knock on my door seeking my business. The only progress I seemed to be making was downward, into a dark, lonely place called self-doubt. I visited this place often, usually from my couch, in a horizontal position.

Fall, winter, and halfway into spring, same story. Zilch. On Good Friday, I had one of my "let's get together for lunch" appointments on my calendar. Had it been anyone other than my friend Kate Larsen, I probably would have canceled. After all, it was a Holy Day.

We were having one of those honest conversations good friends sometimes have, and I confessed to Kate that nothing was happening for me, except that some people had hinted around that they'd like me to consult with them about their business.

"I don't want to be a consultant," I whined. "I want to be a professional speaker."

As any good, wise friend would do, Kate mostly listened. She also had a little gift for me, a book, *The Power of Purpose*, by Richard Lieder.

Just what I needed, another book filled with half-truths and platitudes about purpose, passion, and profits. What I needed was someone to write me a check for something—anything—just so I could feel of value.

Aloud, I politely thanked her and promised to read the book.

As we hugged goodbye, Kate casually asked, "Tell me, Mark, what's wrong with being a consultant?"

"Well, um. . .you know. . .I guess, nothing is wrong with consulting," I stammered.

I went to church for Good Friday services, then home, ate dinner, fell asleep on the couch soon after. It had become a nightly ritual, the after-dinner nap attack. Only this time, when I woke up to go to bed, it was around midnight, and I was wide awake. How would I be able to get back to sleep?

Okay, I'll read that damn little book.

From midnight until daybreak, I read. Something began to turn in my heart and mind. I made some notes, even did several of the exercises. I thought about my purpose all day Saturday. When I had left church on Good Friday, we left in the dark, with the lights turned out, symbolizing Christ being in the tomb. When I went to church on Sunday, I knew the sanctuary would still be dark. There would come that moment, usually during one of the hymns, that the lights would suddenly come on, in magnificent celebration, timed just right to when we would be belting out a jubilant chorus.

Easter morning came a day early for me that year. Jesus rose from the dead, and I rose from, well, the couch, to say the least. Hallelujah, amen.

· · · · · ·

Not long after this holiday weekend, because I was in the habit of going to a certain professional networking meeting, I went again. The excitement of Easter weekend was becoming more of a memory than a motivation, yet at this particular meeting, facing the same group of business people I had faced for the past ten months, I truly seemed to surrender to something. To what or to whom, I did not know.

It was my turn—my minute—to stand up and introduce myself, again. Only this time I didn't blather on about my broad range of services and menu of presentation topics. None of which, you might recall, had I provided to a single client or audience since Small Business (Not-So-Much) Success was born. My calendar was empty from Day One. Instead, I simply got up and shared my dream. In a monotone, mind you, with nary an inflection of enthusiasm whatsoever.

"My name is Mark LeBlanc, and I run a company called Small Business Success. I work with people who want to start a business and with small business owners who want to grow their business." Period, end. I shut up and sat down.

There were about twenty-five business people at this meeting, and when it was over, seven of them came up to me. Now, this was a total surprise, because for ten months, no one—and I mean no one—had any interest in what I did or had to offer. Instead of repelling people, as was my habit, I seemed to be attracting prospects. There was a *line*, for heaven's sake!

"I want to start my own business," said one woman.

"My wife has been wanting to start her own business; give me your card," said a businessman.

"I've been in business ten years, but seem kind of stuck. I'd like to know more about growing my business, cranking it up a notch. Can you help me with that?" came from another.

My favorite response was a friend's: "I've been listening to your introductions for ten months, and I had no clue this is what you do. I think I can refer a few people to you."

Within thirty days, seven prospects wrote me a check and engaged me in the process of helping them start or grow their business. It was as if the floodgates opened and soon prospects came in faster than I could handle. Okay, maybe not that fast, but when you did not earn a nickel for nearly a year, this new-found success felt like I was sipping from a fire hose.

Call me a slow learner, but on that particular morning, instead of talking about my products or my specific services, I had focused on the outcomes of my work:

Start a business.
Grow your business.

I wove those two outcomes into a simple statement, "I work with people who want to start a business and small business owners who want to grow their business," and it became my introduction, always, any time, anywhere. I started teaching my clients how to create a great introduction for themselves and their businesses. I reminded them that in the attraction phase of the marketing and selling process, you have seven to seventeen seconds to get the ear of a prospect. If you can't get his or her ear in that amount of time, it is unlikely you will ever get it. (My ten-month wait being a perfect example.)

I gave it a name—The Defining Statement—and described it as a simple, one-sentence answer to the question, "What do you do?" Over the next three years I identified seven rules, three tests, four tips, eight uses, and twelve formats for creating a killer defining statement based on who your ideal prospect is and what your primary outcomes are. At the time, I didn't know why focusing on outcomes worked so well, just that it did. My clients actually called it genius. The Defining Statement was truly a turning point in my career and in my business.

⊚ ⊚ ⊚ ⊚ ⊚ ⊚

I still have my first copy of *The Greatest Salesman in the World,* the one my dad gave me from his case of them, the same one Og Mandino autographed at my first NSA conference. I always thought that if I ever write a book, I want to write one that people will buy by the case.

So I did. My first book was a little blue paperback you could read in one sitting called *Growing Your Business.* It became, and still is, the core of my speaking business. I still don't have a menu of topics; I have one topic: "Growing Your Business." And I can present that topic in anywhere from thirty minutes to three days. People did, and still do, buy the book by the case.

In fact, I still chuckle at an anonymous review posted on Amazon.com by a guy who characterized my book as "Og Mandino Lite." I took it as a compliment, although I don't think he meant it that way.

It was a few years later, when an unexpected event and someone else's amazing response to that unexpected event prompted what I will always consider to be the book's highest praise.

My dad was sixty-one at the time, still going strong with the two businesses he and my mom owned back in Fertile, Minnesota: LeBlanc Real Estate and Action Advertising. He called me a few weeks before my birthday that year to tell me he had no intention of retiring, that my success had gotten him to thinking that he hadn't quite realized his full potential yet, that he still had at least another ten good years in him, and that he was going to give them everything he's got.

On my birthday, my mom called.

"Your dad has had a stroke."

They were taking him to Altru Hospital in Grand Forks, North Dakota.

What's a stroke? Back then, it was a foreign medical term to me, and there was no time to ask. I cancelled my birthday plans and drove the six hours to Grand Forks. Little did I know that my family's world was about to be rocked to the core.

When we arrived, we went directly to the Intensive Care Unit where everyone had red eyes and could barely talk. It was more serious than earlier imagined, they told us. The danger of losing my best friend was imminent.

I still didn't know what a stroke was.

Within twenty-four hours, I sure did. The doctor called a family meeting and told us in no uncertain terms that Dad was not going to make it, and if by some miracle he did, he would most likely end up in a vegetative state and die in a nursing home.

"You might as well go home now. We'll take care of him from here," the doctor recommended.

Like hell we will. Are you kidding me? This is my dad and best friend you are talking about.

For the next thirty days, we camped out in the waiting room, morning, noon, and night. 24/7/30. We took shifts. We answered approximately thirty calls a day to the waiting room. Friends and relatives came and sat with us. Over five hundred get-well cards flowed in. This was the one and only Ralph LeBlanc, after all.

He loves to tell that story, and not from a nursing home. Although he was paralyzed on the left side of his body, he was still able to drive, play cards, and he even founded a stroke survivors support group in Crookston, Minnesota. But he couldn't work. His dream had died.

Or maybe I should say that it was transplanted.

Not long after my dad returned home, Mom called me in tears and about gave me a heart attack. (I knew what that was.)

She was crying and asked me if I could please loan her $5,000, and she promised profusely between gulps of air that she would pay me back.

"Don't worry about it," I told her, and overnighted her the check.

Back then (it was only thirteen years ago as I write this) in small towns in northern Minnesota, when couples worked together, the man was usually the lead, and my parents' working relationship was no different. My dad was alive, praise God, but their world would never be the same, to put it mildly. My mom had always been second-in-command, and now she was forced to step up to the plate and assume 100 percent responsibility for their new lot in life.

But this was Lois LeBlanc, up against the wall and soon-to-be another small business success story. She was sixty years old and—I would assume—scared to death, although she never let on. She was simply embarrassed to call her son for a loan.

She had two businesses to deal with, and her first decision was easy: dial one down. She cherry-picked a few of the plum clients, but otherwise closed the advertising business.

She focused on the real estate business. And in those ten years that my dad wanted to give it his all, she quadrupled the business. Yes, it's true. Every word of it. Plus, she paid off the mortgage, became debt free, and put more than $100,000 away for retirement. She bought a new car and paid cash for it. She paid me back the $5,000. I didn't ask for it, but it was hugely important to her to make that payment.

My mom achieved all this success in her sixties, while she was taking care of Dad, who required a fair amount of care. She did it while she helped take care of her mother, my grandma Ruby, who died after a three-year lingering illness.

Did I mention Mom's kidney transplant? She had one at the age of sixty-four, which meant accomplishing all this in between going to and from dialysis appointments three times a week. Even a kidney transplant didn't slow her down.

Of course, we are all proud of her and no one more so than Dad. In fact, my dad never misses an opportunity to remind us all that he is the luckiest man in the world, and that Mom is the reason for it.

One day, I finally gathered the nerve to ask her.

"How did you do it, Mom? How did you manage to do all of what you did, under the most extreme and challenging circumstances, at a time of life most people are thinking about retiring?"

She looked at me, as only a mother can look at her son.

"I read your book," she said, and her eyes teared up.

"What?" I was dumbfounded.

"I read your book," she repeated. "I didn't understand half of what you wrote, but I did learn one thing. If someone is not interested in what I have to offer or sell, I realize now that it is not about me. So I don't waste time worrying about it. I move on to the next one."

My eyes teared up, too, at what I now consider to be the highest possible praise for anything I have ever done. And she meant it that way.

⊛ ⊛ ⊛ ⊛ ⊛ ⊛

My good friend Francis Bologna called and said he had something to share with me.

"Mark, I want you to consider joining me in a men's retreat put on by the Jesuit religious order."

"Okay, I'm in," I said.

"What? I haven't told you about it yet," he said.

I figure when you have a close friend like Francis, and that friend suggests you do something, you do it. Plus, I was familiar with the history of the men's retreats that the Jesuits put on in retreat centers around the world, fifty-two weekends a year, year in and year out. I just hadn't attended one yet.

And so began my annual sojourn to the little town of Convent, Louisiana, about an hour outside of New Orleans, typically the third weekend of March. Approximately 110 men ages eighteen to eighty-eight attend this annual retreat on this weekend. It became one of my annual benchmarks, and I seldom miss a year.

The Jesuit religious order began conducting these retreats decades ago, and little has changed in the structure of the weekend. It is a silent retreat where no one talks to anyone. Everyone listens to God. You can go on a vacation to rest your body and your mind. However, to rest your soul, you need silence.

The grand silence begins on Thursday evening and ends on Sunday afternoon. It is a special experience, profound for many reasons, and it is unlikely I will ever give it up. Francis has been going for thirty-five years. His father, Gaeton, who passed away several years ago, went every March for fifty-two years. It's now become a family tradition with Francis's son Pete, brother Ricky, nephews, and sons-in-law all making the trip as well. I've become a part of the family, and I made arrangements one year for my dad to join the crew as well. At the end of the retreat, we are all asked to make a contribution and pay what we can afford.

After attending the retreat for several years, I pondered the application of doing something like it in the business world. My peers thought I was crazy. Still, it begged for consideration, and I kept my thoughts, ideas, and feelings to myself.

You see, at the time, a number of very smart marketing and business development experts were conducting weekend seminars they dubbed "Boot Camps." Essentially, they would charge a lot of money, gather as many business owners as they could, flood them with information, load them up with workbooks, give them hand cramps from taking notes, and inundate them with the sheer volume of content, and hope that something would stick. Too often, attendees left overwhelmed, confused, and very few applied much of what they learned. And because the investment was so high, they were reluctant to admit that not much had changed in their business or professional practice.

One of my friends and mentors, Lyman K. (Manny) Steil, Ph.D., told me that when everyone is going one way, think about going the opposite way. I began to play with the idea of conducting the Anti-Boot Camp. What might that look like? What if I created a weekend seminar that contained some anti-boot camp elements, as well as drew upon some of the elements of my annual silent retreat, and even my Teens Encounter Christ experiences? Was it possible that it might have some appeal in the marketplace?

Just as I do when I work with other business owners, I put myself into my own hot seat. Mark, look into the crystal ball and start from scratch. What would you want it to look like? How would it work?

I began to sketch out my three-day business development weekend retreat and named it "The Achievers Circle." My ten founding characteristics were

1) No long sessions.

2) No products or services would be sold.

3) Limit it to a small number of attendees.

4) No workbook or handouts.

5) Focused, with plenty of humor.

6) Provide a special, celebratory dinner.

7) Give each weekend a number.

8) Plenty of breaks.

9) Allow attendees an opportunity to speak.

10) Pass the hat; no formal registration fee.

It was March 17, 2000, when I sat down at my computer and drafted a two-page promotional letter inviting people to a special weekend business experience or retreat. It took me three hours to write the letter, and the same letter was used for nine years and ninety-five weekends before it was finally revised and put into a new format.

I looked at the calendar, selected three weekends, and took a deep breath. I began to fax and email the letter to a number of speech and workshop attendees who had filled out evaluation forms. I was so lacking in confidence that I only invited those people who had given me perfect scores on my evaluations. I said a little prayer and began to send.

Within twenty-four hours, two people had registered and on the first weekend of April, I held my first Achievers Circle and never looked back. At press time 2010, I will have completed more than one hundred Achievers Circles, and the ten founding characteristics have not changed. While many have tried to get me to make changes, I have held firm. I read once that when something is good, it will get better if you stick with it. If it is not good, chances are it will begin to fade and fizzle before ultimately it fails.

The Achievers Circle was, and still is, the most fun I have in my work, and it is quite possibly the most influential work of my career. Even now, as I look back at the Defining Statement, *Growing Your Business,* and Achievers Circle, I realize and believe they were all divinely inspired. I'm just not smart enough to think of this stuff on my own.

Frequently Asked Questions

Why did you do the Camino?

I learned from other walkers along the way that it's commonly said that you do not choose to walk the Camino. The Camino chooses you. That's exactly how I felt from the day I heard about it at my brother's dining room table. I just knew I had to do it. I knew that I would be better for having done so, in so many ways.

One of them being that after completing the Camino, there is not a challenge that is outside of my reach. When I find myself stuck or faced with an obstacle, I think, "If I can walk five hundred miles across Spain, I can do this." My sense of urgency in achieving a particular something has given way to finding my own pace and staying the course. That comes from the Camino, because on the Camino you have two choices every morning: walk or quit. The Camino eventually helps you find your pace.

Frequently Asked Questions

How did you get in shape?

To prepare physically, I walked five miles a day beginning at 5:00 a.m. nearly every day for sixty days just prior to leaving. You can't prepare mentally. Or at least I didn't/couldn't because I had no idea what to expect.

Did you have a plan for how many miles per day you needed to walk?

I had my map and a return ticket from Madrid on October 13. I did have to do some rudimentary math in deciding just how long I would be gone to cover five hundred miles, so, yes, from that standpoint I knew would need to average more than sixteen miles per day if I was going to complete five hundred miles in thirty-one days.

So how many miles did you average?

Here are my stats. The first ten days, I averaged thirteen miles per day. I found myself on gravel roads, paved roads, and cow paths, in ravines, over ancient bridges, mountain passes, and through fields of wheat, corn, sunflowers, and grapes.

Days eleven through twenty were across the flat plains of the *meseta*. It was dry, hot, and boring. Many people struggle through this period even though their bodies are getting decidedly stronger. It didn't bother me, since I was able to now extend my daily distances to eighteen to twenty-two miles per day.

I read that for the average walker, whatever average is, five hundred miles is the equivalent of 1,023,000 steps. But the Camino was no average walk, not with all the up and down steep inclines and rocky paths, so there were many stretches that I was inching along with baby steps. And I stopped counting on Day Two. A million steps are a million steps, give or take thirty thousand here and there.

All said and done, I figure I averaged about 2.5 miles per hour.

What did you eat?

Every day I walked through various remote farming villages, as well as the larger cities of Pamplona, Burgos, Leon, and Ponferrada, so it was simple to buy food and water along the way. Coca-cola became my guilty pleasure, and soon I considered it the nectar of the gods. A Coke and a chocolate croissant could sustain me for miles.

In the evening, I could partake of a pilgrim's meal served up by one of the local bar-restaurant establishments for about €9 euro or $16 U.S. I got a bottle of wine, water, bread, two courses, and dessert. The food was good and plentiful, but heavy, so I would eat the pilgrim's meal about every third or fourth night.

While I enjoyed the local Spanish breads, meats, and cheeses, my favorite was *ensalada mixta*, the Spanish version of a chef's salad, only much better, I must say.

In the refugios, *how do Camino couples . . . oh, never mind.*
They find a hotel, if they're not too tired.

Did you walk every single day?
No, I took two days off. After ten days, I went off the trail and
checked into a two-star hotel in Burgos. (Alone.) It was about
$50 U.S. and a luxurious experience by any star measurement.
I needed a mental, emotional, and physical break and decided
that a day off after ten days, and then again after twenty days
would be a welcome relief.

After twenty days, I took another day off and spent the night
in Ponferrada. I checked into a hotel next door to a McDonald's.
Yes, that McDonald's. If Coke was the nectar of the gods, a Big
Mac was comfort food from on high. I ate three meals during
the next twenty-four hours with Ronald McDonald.

Did you pray along the way?
No, very little. You are in way too much pain to pray. The walk
itself becomes your prayer. As each day went by, I felt myself—
dare I say my burden—getting lighter.

Did you make new friends along the way?
I met a lot of great people along the way from all over the world,
although not many from the United States. I met, walked with,
ate with, and laughed with people from Germany, Canada, Korea,

Italy, Ireland, England, Holland, Brazil, Japan, Australia, France, Austria, and other great nations.

A funny thing about the Camino is that when you met someone along the way, you never knew how long that person would walk with you, or even sit with you, let alone whether they'd ever be a part of your life or whether you would even see that person again. Suddenly, your hellos and your good-byes were meaningful in a way you could not have imagined. Living in the moment and being fully present were no longer clichés.

How did you know where to go each day?
Yellow arrows marked the Camino, but they appeared in various shapes and materials. Many times it was like living in a page out of *Where's Waldo?*

I also had a written guide. Here's an example from Day Twenty-five, which covered twenty-four kilometers.

Route from Ponferrada to Villafranca del Bierzo
The pilgrims´ route leads down *calle* Mateo Garza to the bridge over the river Sil, crosses it, and continues along the Carretera de Madrid. A few meters further on, the Paseo Huertas del Sacramento leads off to the right along the river until it crosses the railway track and passes the slag heap of the electrical power plant of Compostilla on the left. You then cross the Bajo Bierzo canal and carry on into Compostilla, passing the parish church on the left. On reaching Columbrianos, which, like Compostilla, is a

suburb of Ponferrada, you emerge onto the Villablino road, only to bear left off of it a few meters down along *calle de las Eras*, also known as the Camino Real. After going through a tunnel underneath the railway track, you soon come out onto the road to Vega de Espinareda and, a couple of kilometers later, past houses and vegetable patches, reach Fuentes Nuevas. After following the Calle Real through the village, you continue on through fertile farmland to Camponaraya, just over a kilometer away. In Camponaraya, follow the road to the outskirts of the village, where you take a path on the left opposite a wine-growing cooperative. After following the path through vineyards, you reach a low, flat hilltop, after which the path drops down into the pretty Arroyo Magaz valley, crosses the river and runs through a leafy riverside wood until it crosses the road. On the far side, you continue down a farm track through vineyards and then up a small hill, before dropping into Cimadevila, from where you enter Cacabelos along the Calle de los Peregrinos. The N-VI leads out of Cacabelos and across a bridge over the river Cua, passing the beautiful Chapel of Nuestra Senora de las Angustias on the right. Two km later, you come to Pieros passing the hilltop ruins of Castrum Bergidium. At km 406.8, bear right off the road along a path, which, after crossing the Arroyo de los Valtuilles stream, narrows through dense vegetation before leading out onto a wider track known as the Camino de la Virgen, coming from Valtuille de Arriba. Less than two km from there, you reach the Iglesia de Santiago at the entrance of Villafranca del Bierzo.

What was your favorite day?

As it turns out, I just gave you my marching orders for my favorite day. It was the kind of day that dreams are all about. I left Ponferrada late morning. The weather was perfect, the landscape surreal, and it was harvest day for grape growers. I walked through acres of grape fields filled with both plump, juicy grapes and grape-picking people. Farmers were bringing loads of green and purple grapes into the wineries by the truck and trailer load.

As I walked through one small village around 3:00 p.m., a Spanish man stopped me and asked me if I wanted to take a break with his family and have a glass of wine. At least I think that's what he said, because the only word I understood was *vino*. Who could resist?

I took my backpack off and joined them as they took a break from harvest and we shared a bottle of wine. And then when he offered me a refill, I held out my glass. He laughed and poured me a larger glass. When we had finished, I took his picture and went on my way.

This was one of those days, that if you were walking with someone you loved and who loved you, it might be the best day of your life.

What was your worst day?

Turns out that my first day was not the worst; I downgraded it to a whopping big surprise. The worst day was Day Thirty-two, my second-to-last day. I awoke on Day Thirty-two knowing I would reach Monte de Gozo, the City of Joy, that evening. The good people of Santiago created a huge, compound-type village there, where up to eight hundred pilgrims can stay overnight free and prepare to walk the final six kilometers into Santiago the next morning. I felt stronger than ever on Day Thirty-one and knew that today would be an easy, eight-to-ten-hour day with breaks. I figured I would get into Monte de Gozo around dinner time.

During the last ten days or so, you begin to see the Latin word *Ultreia* hand painted on buildings, signs, rocks, trees, and even the occasional dumpster. *Ultreia* means keep going. Every time you saw this graffiti art, it seemed like the millions of pilgrims that had walked this path throughout the last one thousand years were cheering you on, patting you on the back, and high-fiving you as you walked along your way. I began to realize this was hallowed ground and not simply one of the world's great hikes. I was no longer a walker. I felt like a pilgrim. My destination was almost in sight. I knew I would never be the same. And I panicked.

You see, it is human nature to quit, to throw in the towel. We make and keep commitments to others, but more often, the majority of commitments we make and then break are to ourselves. We quit diets. We quit exercising. We quit on friends.

We quit ourselves. We quit relationships. We quit careers. We quit our dreams. We quit God.

Or we start something and never finish it—a kissing cousin to quitting because we don't actually quit, yet we do make a mental promise that of course we will get back to whatever it was we didn't finish some other day, when the time is right. Yeah, right. That day never comes, but we give ourselves a reprieve from feeling like we quit something again, even though we did. We're good at getting 80 or 90 percent done and then not having the time, energy, or creativity to wrap a ribbon around it and be done with it. Or, we get 90 percent of the way and lack the courage to say, "Yes!" and move forward.

On Day Thirty-two, as close as I was to the finish line, as strong as I was physically, my mind began to sabotage my steps. I was reminded of how many things I had started and never finished. I was reminded of how many times I quit on something or someone.

Every step I took that day seemed like I had an additional ten pounds wrapped around each ankle. It was agonizing, and I wanted to quit.

If only I could borrow a bike. Maybe I have walked enough and should reward myself with a taxi ride the final distance. No one would ever know, would they?

Yes, someone would know. I would always know.

I checked into the largest *refugio* of the Camino that evening and spent the rest of the night in silence.

CHAPTER FIVE

The Slide

The second time I appeared on stage in my underwear was in front of two-thousand-plus convention-goers in New York City. I was forty-seven years old and president of the National Speakers Association.

I suppose it might be called making an entrance, and other NSA presidents have arrived on stage at their national convention on horseback or straddling a Harley. It's kind of a big moment everyone waits for. Me—I slid across the stage in my stocking feet, wearing a long-sleeved, button-down white shirt and boxers. No fig leaf or angel's harps playing in the background à la my seventh-grade role as Adam. Instead, I donned dark sunglasses à la Tom Cruise in the movie *Risky Business*, with Bob Seger's "Old Time Rock 'n' Roll" blaring.

My welcome speech lasted eighteen seconds and consisted of two words. It went long because the crowd was screaming so loud that I had to stand there in my underwear and wait for the din to die down so that I could deliver my two-word speech. "NSA Rocks!"

Again, the crowd went wild. The stage lights went dark. I put my pants back on, and the record-breaking 2008 National Convention of the National Speakers Association was underway.

Context?

Each year the president of NSA creates a theme for his or her reign. Themes have run the gamut, from nice to poignant, from catchy to pathetic. (Same goes for logos.)

In coming up with the theme for my year as president, my team and I bantered around the notion that whatever theme we settled on, we wanted it to celebrate the speaking profession, not merely turn a phrase or coin a catch word. We wanted it to move the masses. Whether old school or new school, NSA was their school. Close, but too long. At some point we reminded ourselves of our internal mantra that our year would definitely be "a lot less Hallmark and a whole lot more rock and roll." Hmm.

NSA Rocks.

Simple. Clear. Compelling. It was focused on them, the profession, the industry, the organization, not us.

Once we added the flames, it was perfect. It became the battle cry, the banner that would be carried and brought to life at every turn. Best of all, people could—and did—dance to it. Or in my case, slide to it.

Little did I know back in 1984, when I used half of my $3,000 business loan to go to the National Speakers Association Convention in San Francisco, that Maxine McIntyre, the woman who introduced me to Og Mandino, was a prophet. She told me "Mark, some day you will be president of NSA."

At first I thought she said that to all the new kids in the club, but turns out she didn't. Turns out she was right, and not just on the national scale. I was also elected president of the Minnesota chapter, then later to the national board of directors in 2001, and was named vice president in 2005. In the world of NSA, that means a year as VP, a year as president-elect, and then my presidential term that ran July 2007 through August 2008.

Here's the thing about NSA. If I were to do a genealogy of my friends, relationships, and fondest memories—all things good in my life—98.7 percent connect directly to someone or something in NSA. If I could get my friend Dr. John, to start a speaking career and join NSA, it would be 100 percent.

I practically grew up in the Minnesota chapter, and it is there that I trace my greatest accomplishments and highest honors. In 1997, they created the Mark LeBlanc Award for Outstanding Service, which is given annually to a hard-working (on a volunteer basis, mind you) chapter member. I was inducted into the

NSA Minnesota Speakers Hall of Fame in 2006, and recently an anonymous member of the Minnesota chapter contributed a humbling sum of money to have an official coin minted that commemorated my year of service as the NSA national president. There are no degrees, designations, abbreviations, or anything more I need to earn or be awarded than those three honors.

⊛　⊛　⊛　⊛　⊛　⊛

Here's another thing about NSA. It's not a small business, by any means. Yet the lessons of leadership are, for the most part, the same as they would be regardless of business size or shape, whether you're leading a small business, family business, Fortune 500 corporation, association, chamber of commerce, parish council, or school board. Leadership is leadership.

I don't know what brand of leadership styles you subscribe to, but I found that when it came to leading a group of 3,600 professional speakers, authors, and consultants (who all seemed to have an opinion and were never at a loss for sharing it), leadership styles ran the gamut. Some leaders were vanilla, and some were spumoni; some were calm and collected, and others were hot-headed; some were selfless, and others were self-absorbed. Some wanted it for the right reasons, and some wanted it for the wrong ones.

Bottom line for me was that I saw a lot and learned a lot from each and every style—the proverbial good, bad, and ugly. Here are my seven lessons on leadership, some long, some short, learned the LeBlanc way (which is not necessarily the easiest way).

1.

Stand for something, even if it's not universally accepted.
I raised a ruckus right after being installed as president in July of 2007, all because I took a stand in my inaugural speech, possibly the most important ten-minute speech of my life. At least that is how I prepared for it. Shortly after being appointed vice president, I studied the twenty greatest speeches of the last one hundred years for wisdom and insight into how great leaders influence others. I wanted my year as president to be a strong call to return to the art of professional speaking and to remind our members of the impact and influence we have, both personally and professionally. Speakers touch hearts, engage minds, and stir souls, regardless of audience size or topic.

"Professional speakers join NSA for two reasons, and two reasons only," I said from the stage. "Because they want to speak more or because they want to speak better. That's it.

"But, in the last few years we seem to have gone away from that, and it has become unfashionable to be a speaker. We are fast becoming a melting pot of people who don't want to speak much anymore. We want to stay home and make money in our jammies. If you want to stay home and make money in your jammies, great. Maybe you should join the Make Money in Your Jammies Association.

"Let me remind you. We are the National Speakers Association. We are not the National Consultants Association, the National Coaches Association, the National Writers Association, and contrary to what some would have you believe, we are not the National Information Marketing Association.

"Not that there is anything wrong with any of these revenue vehicles. And NSA will continue to provide you with programming to help you in these areas. But we are the National Speakers Association, and it's time to be proud of being a professional speaker, again."

The crowd went wild.

But apparently a few vocal people (coaches, consultants, writers, and information marketers, perhaps?) didn't hear or tuned out that last part when I specifically said there was nothing wrong with any of those endeavors; I just wanted professional speakers to be proud of their calling and not feel "less than" in any way. I wanted them to realize that there is no such thing as being quote-unquote "just a speaker." Leaders take a stand, carry a big banner, and make it stick.

2.

Surround yourself with the best team,
and swing for the fences.

It is human nature to want to leave your thumbprint, make a mark, a significant contribution of some kind, whether it's on a particular project or an entire organization. NSA is no different. Every leadership team comes in wanting to have the best conference, or the best magazine, the best theme, or the best whatever for the last thirty-five years. "How can we tweak this or that, make it even better than the year before?" Not a bad objective, to be sure. You don't have to be sick to get better.

I began recruiting my leadership team the day after I was appointed vice president. (I still had two years before I would be president.) The president names approximately thirty people to positions that range from a committee chairperson to honorary member of the board of directors for a one-year term. If three points determine a plane (and they do), then three people determined my primary leadership team: meetings and convention chair, *Speaker* magazine editorial advisory board chair, and *Voices of Experience* audio CD chair. These positions would be charged with bringing my vision to life in tangible ways, through the most visible touch points during the year.

I did not look for people who would create the best convention, meetings, magazine, or VOE series of the last thirty-five years. I looked for people who would create the best convention, meetings, magazine, and VOE for the next thirty-five years. Think about that. I needed three people who could step up to the plate and swing for the fences each and every time. Three people who wouldn't settle for merely making a mark on their area of responsibility, but rather, three people who wanted to make a difference and make it mean something beyond their year of service.

Eric Chester, meetings and conventions; Terri Langhans, *Speaker* magazine; and Bill Stainton, *Voices of Experience* audio CD program—what a team. I trusted them with my vision, and now, with my life. That's the kind of team a leader needs to succeed.

3.

Focus on what you can do,

not on what you could do if conditions were perfect.

Stop whining, waiting, wishing, or hoping that the stars will align, that things (or people) will magically change. Do something—anything—that moves you closer to your dream, mission, target, result, objective, or destination. And do it regardless of how you feel that day, in spite of how So-And-So let you down (or stabbed you in the back), whether you've got a budget or not. Make the call. Reach out one more time. Go anyway. When you can't change the conditions, change your response to them.

4.

Keep your fun meter on MAX.

Don't take yourself too seriously, your attitude is contagious.

5.

Say something nice to everyone you meet.

Every time you're with someone, say something nice. Why? In the words of the late, great NSA President Ira Hayes, "You'll be a super star!"

6.

Lean on those who care about you unconditionally.

Leaders don't have all the answers. They aren't expected to. But they do know where—and when—to go when they need help. I'm not talking about knowing where to go for an answer, because sometimes there is no answer. There were times that I just needed a new perspective, a different way of looking at a situation, challenge, or crisis. And sometimes I needed that fresh perspective at midnight, or I needed to vent first, or cuss a little (or a lot). And I knew who would be there for me, who would listen, tell me what I needed to hear, whether I wanted to hear it or not, and not tell a word to anyone else on the planet. Ever.

7.

When it's over, say good-bye.

Ira Hayes also said, "Everything ends." He wasn't talking about death, but he could have been. He wasn't talking about good times or bad times, but he could have been. He wasn't necessarily talking about business challenges either, but he could have been. On one level, it could be as simple as "when the prospect says 'yes,' stop selling." When you find yourself in a hole, stop digging. Don't beat a dead horse. When the project is completed, mission accomplished (or even abandoned), move on.

Remember my TEC days (Teens Encounter Christ)? I was the TEC guy for three years, speaking at retreats, attracting participants, recruiting volunteers, expanding the reach and scope of the program all over the state of Minnesota. When I graduated and moved away, and then moved back, the TEC folks were elated. "He's back! Hallelujah!"

Not so fast. I still believed in TEC, and I still encouraged people to attend and to volunteer. But there was new leadership, and I had my own dream to pursue. I would be in the way, a voice from the past, albeit a rather recent past, someone who would more than likely dilute the direction of the organization than advance it.

But lots of leaders have trouble saying good-bye, literally and figuratively. They hang around, lobby behind the scenes, cling to unfinished business or unfulfilled outcomes, and try to push them through sideways if they can. As president of NSA, my term ended August 5, 2008. When it's over, say good-bye. And that's exactly what I did.

I left for Spain four weeks later.

THE CAMINO

There Is No Finish Line

I have no clue what it's like to be a bride on her wedding day, but Romantic Mark imagines her awakening that morning (if she slept at all) with a range of emotions from excitement to fear to relief, perhaps with a measure of regret, that it will soon be over.

"At last! It's here. The Big Day." Brides, graduating seniors, marathon runners, and Camino pilgrims, they have that in common.

I awoke from my reflective night of silence on Day Thirty-three to loud, boisterous laughter. It was everywhere. The Big Day had arrived for every single one of us, and the rush of everyone getting ready to leave charged the air with anticipation and excitement. No wonder they called it the City of Joy. I decided to take my time. Santiago was only six kilometers away and just a bit of a stroll into the city to the glorious Cathedral, where the journey would end.

I showered, dressed, and dumped the contents of my backpack onto my cot to edit and lighten my load one last time. I sorted through the items I didn't want to drag back to Minnesota, things I wouldn't need, or ever want to see again even if I did need them.

I dropped my dirty socks and reached for my telescoping, collapsible walking poles when I heard the woman scream. I spun around, wielding the wrong end of one of them to use as a weapon or, well, maybe a bug squisher. Screaming Mimi, as I had instantly nicknamed her, was coming right at me, wildly waving her arms as if she were trying to stop a bus. I lowered my weapon, dropped it back on the cot, stepped into the aisle, and opened my arms wide.

We had met on Day One at the *refugio*, if you call awkwardly trying to learn how to pronounce someone's name meeting. She was German and spoke no English. My name is easy in just about every language; hers was not. I politely tried to communicate with her a brief time, but no luck. Seeing her again in the City of Joy, I was reminded (and a bit ashamed) of my first impression of her: overweight and unattractive with what appeared to be a permanently attached chip on her shoulder and a perpetual posture of despair.

I saw her again a few days later as I was walking through a city park in Pamplona. She was sitting alone on a bench, face in her hands, crying. I stopped, and tried to connect with her, but no such luck. All I could do was give her a smile and wish her well by repeating the mantra of the Pilgrims, *Buen Camino*. I walked away feeling pity for her, and thought, *there's one who won't make it.*

I never thought about her again, until there she was, running full-bore, straight at me. She was crying again, but this time I could see they were tears of pure joy. She threw her arms around me, wrapped them tight, and would not let go. I'm sure if she had said "*Danka shern*," à la Wayne Newton's preferred spelling, I would have understood her. But the embrace said it better.

I stepped back and looked at her. It was as if she had been touched by God's magic wand and was transformed right before my eyes. I was stunned. Her smile was nothing short of glorious. Her amazing heart, a lighter, brighter countenance was there for all to see. The chip was gone, and it was I who was the lucky one to have seen her that morning.

I never did get her name, and I know I will never see her again, yet we shared a moment of joy, complete with laughter, tears, and gratitude.

And then it dawned on me, what did I look like, how had I changed?

        ◦   ◦   ◦   ◦   ◦   ◦

I gathered what little remained of my possessions and hoisted my backpack up for the last time and started the last leg of my walk into Santiago de Compostela. After a short spell, I stopped for coffee and my last chocolate croissant. Make that two chocolate croissants. The end was near, and I was ready to rejoice and celebrate. I walked the last three kilometers and arrived in the square in front of the Cathedral of Santiago.

I'm here! This was it, the big moment. Or was it? The square was nearly empty. No banners, no confetti, no nothing. No Camino-clad volunteers handing out water, granola bars, or bananas. Surely, there would be some form of welcoming committee? A high five or at least a "Praise God!"?

Maybe the finish line was a few more blocks? I walked around the Cathedral looking for a sign, one more arrow showing me where the party was, where to complete my pilgrimage.

I circled back to the center of the square, looked up at the massive front door of the Cathedral and realized I was most certainly in the right place. I had walked five hundred miles, alone, and had, indeed, reached my destination, with only one person there to acknowledge the accomplishment—me.

I was stunned. I realized in that moment that I would never again need anyone else to cheer me on—for anything—ever. I realized that I was, indeed, more than enough.

Then a joy of the deepest and purest kind began to run through me like nothing I had ever experienced. Everything I carried in my heart, all the worries, the regrets, and the baggage from the night before—from forever ago—they were completely gone. Everything was released, replaced with joy, peace, and gratitude that permeated my very soul. After more than a million steps, the longest walk of a lifetime, I would never be the same.

I realized that Santiago was not my destination after all, and that my arrival at the Cathedral square was not the end.

There is no finish line. And my need for one? I let that go.

Never Be the Same

Months after I returned from the Camino, I was telling my dad about the lack of fanfare, the literal (and metaphoric) lack of a finish line at the Cathedral, and how there was no one there to cheer me on or recognize my accomplishment. I shared with him what a powerful lesson it was for me, and he put it better than I could.

"Mark, you didn't need anyone to cheer you on. The band was playing inside. You remember that, and you can do anything," he said.

He is right. Whenever I think of it, Frank Sinatra's "My Way," my favorite song, plays in my head.

What is "Your Way?" What is your dream? Are you on the path or on the bench?

I discovered one of my dreams in December 1982—to be a professional speaker. The path was not an easy one. I think I quit a thousand times. Fortunately, for me, I recommitted myself 1,001 times. If I had not, I would not be doing the good work I feel called and compelled to do. I would not be using the God-given talents I was blessed with. I certainly would not have had the privilege of serving as a leader and president of the prestigious National Speakers Association. I most definitely would not be having the kind of impact and influence with the people I serve best.

In *The Greatest Miracle in the World*, Og Mandino's sequel to *The Greatest Salesman in the World*, he wrote about the pilot light that each of us has inside. The light burns brightly for some, and for others it's a mere flicker or nigh onto extinguished. Along the way to achieving our dream, running our race, living our lives, we allow our mistakes, failures, circumstances, and decisions to get the best of us. When we do, our spirit weakens and our resolve fades, but our pilot light never goes out. It's there, if only a glimmer, until we die.

Please don't ask me why, but at some point early on, I dedicated my life to brightening the pilot light in each of you, whether through my presentations, coaching, books—even Facebook. It may seem a bit crazy, but it's true. I am not sure why I believe in you, but I do.

And at those times when my pilot light burned dim, I held on to my faith in God, my faith in my family, my faith in my friends, and my faith in myself. I knew there was something in there burning to be shared and that it could impact a person's life, work, or career. I held on to that. I held on to the people who had faith in me and believed in my work, even when I did not. I didn't quit.

Unlike achieving goals and having the feelings fade, the lessons learned from the Camino live with me every day, and my life gets richer and more blessed. I have never been happier or more at peace. I am still hard at work, and the challenges and obstacles still surface, but my response to them is quite different.

No matter what your current situation is, good or not-so-good, hang in there. Miracles do happen, memories can be healed, and dreams do come true. Make a commitment to yourself first, not to the finish line. Celebrate the effort, and remember what Judith told me Day One on my Camino, "You can always take another step."

You can take another one, too. Deliberately, in the direction of your dream. It may be a baby step, but you can take one. Today. Tomorrow, and the next day.

Share your story. Let your light shine. And the world will never be the same.

Ultreia!

MANY TO BE THANKFUL FOR

My dad is my best friend. My mom is my true inspiration. Sherry is in a category of one. Cathy is a living angel on earth. My brother, John, models for me what it means to be a good man and a great dad.

My nieces and nephews, named in the dedication, light the way for me each and every single day. Just the thought of them gives me hope that the world indeed has a brighter future ahead.

Thank you to all of my individual consulting and coaching clients, as well as to every single person who has attended an Achievers Circle. Your faith in me and belief in my work is invaluable.

To Terri Langhans, CSP, who listened carefully, responded appropriately, and helped me shape my story beyond anything I could ever have imagined.

I'll never forget Eric Chester, CSP, CPAE, Bill Stainton, and another round of applause for Terri Langhans, CSP, who, along with me, created the NSA Rocks band and top leadership team. Might I add, it was the greatest leadership team in the history of the National Speakers Association.

My best to my friends in Fertile, my classmates at Crosier Seminary, and my neighbors in the National Speakers Association, I will always remember you fondly and with much thanks and gratitude.

And anyone else who thinks they should have been included here. . .well, you know who you are, and thank you!

On grandma and grandpa Rude's farm east of Fertile (1969).

With my dad in Manitoba, Canada (1970).

Fish story gets bigger! Salmon fishing in Alaska (1996).

*With Dad and Mom, at my high school graduation
from Crosier Seminary Prep School (1979).*

*With Maxine McIntyre at the NSA convention
in San Francisco (1983).*

With Og Mandino and Maxine McIntyre,
holding Og's book of Ten Scrolls (1983).

Running the show at my printing company,
in Columbia Heights, Minnesota (1988).

Left to Right: with Joan Kennedy and Priscilla "Tootie" Nelson (1991).

With my mom, a small business success story in her own right (2000).

Lois and Ralph LeBlanc (2007).

The NSA Rocks Band, left to right, Eric Chester, CSP, CPAE; Terri Langhans, CSP; Mark; and Bill Stainton (2007).

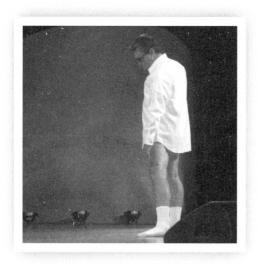

The Slide: NSA Convention, New York City, and the second time I appeared on stage in my underwear (2008).

Mark LeBlanc (2009).

ABOUT TERRI LANGHANS, CSP

Terri is the author of *The 7 Marketing Mistakes Every Business Makes (And How to Fix Them)* and former CEO of a national ad agency and marketing firm that she started from scratch and sold to a publicly traded Big Boy. She named her speaking business Blah Blah Blah because she's all about helping people be less ordinary and more effective communicators. And because it's funny.

She attended her first NSA meeting in 1998, and Mark was the first speaker she heard. After attending his Achiever's Circle #8, her life has never been the same. She earned the Certified Speaking Professional designation for one reason and one reason only. Because she wanted Mark LeBlanc, as president of NSA, to be the one to hang the medal around her neck. And he did.

www.BlahBlahBlah.us

ABOUT MARK LEBLANC

Mark had a job once for about six months and found out at an early age that he was unemployable. At twenty-two, he embarked on his entrepreneurial journey and has owned several small businesses. He now speaks and writes on the core issues that entrepreneurs and professionals face on a daily basis. He is the architect of a unique business development philosophy that has been embraced by small businesses as well as major corporations around North America. Mark is a past president of the National Speakers Association and was inducted into the Minnesota Speakers Association Hall of Fame in 2006. He is an avid walker, practices hot yoga, and is a great uncle to his nieces and nephews.

www.MarkLeBlanc.com